Blossoms Gathered At Dusk

Blossoms Gathered at Dusk
By Madame Li Huarui
Compiled by Ben Wu

Cover design by Anya Kholodova

Copyright 2009 © Ben Wu

ISBN: 978-0-578-03137-8

All rights rserved, which includes the right to reproduce this book or portions thereof in any form whatsoever except as provided by the U.S. Copyright Law

Lovingly dedicated to
Madam Chew Hoe Eng 周慧英
And her devoted son,
Vincent Lai 賴榮順

Table of Contents

Foreword by Chelsea Flattery

Author's Note

Always Hopeful

Be Thankful

Thoughts on Being One Hundred

Sweet Memories

Change

The Nine Joys of Being Old

Cherish

Romantic Love

A Simple Meal

Peace of Mind

Suicide

The Power of Affection

Thoughts on God

A Discourse on the Christian Bible

What Is Right?

Contemplating a Portrait of Kwan Yin

Thoughts Recorded After Attending a Holy Ghost Revival

Thoughts for the New Year

Spring

Summer

Autumn

Winter

Ruminations on Holidays

Advice to a Troubled Friend

The Subject of Race

An Angel

A Letter from a Friend

Thoughts on Calligraphy

Poetry

The Summer House of Infinite Joy

An Inscription

Expounding the Classics

Final Thoughts from Madame Li

Acknowledgments

A Note from Ben Wu

Foreword

By Chelsea Flattery

What can one say about Madame Li that hasn't already been said? As a woman who has seen one hundred years come and go, there are few whose insight into the world is as vast and meaningful. Madame Li is a painter and calligrapher, as well as a frequent diarist and poet. Living in relative seclusion somewhere in the United States, Madame Li has all the time in the world to ponder life's great mysteries; she is a keen follower of Buddhism, Christianity, and Taoism. Her insight into issues both present and past makes her a constant fount of advice and occasional humor. There are few others who could write about the varied topics contained within this book as Madame Li. The following text is a collection of her writings, from anecdotes about her own life, advice to her readers, and her own thoughts about the great literary classics. She discusses a wide assortment of topics, including the seasons, love, death, God, suicide, romance, and art. The words inside this book have proven to be most influential, comforting, humorous, and astute. As the saying goes, to hold a book by Madame Li is to hold in your hand the understanding of the world.

Author's Note

My dear children, I, with the help of friends, have attempted to put down in writing some of my ramblings. I am an old woman, now nearing my 101st birthday, and have long been considered silly. So, take my advice lightly and seek not any profound truths in my words. Merely enjoy the characters and tales I feebly try to bring to life in the texts that lie hereafter.
    Humbly

Madame Li Huarui

Written July 2009 Autumn Recluse Cottage

Always Hopeful

Written for the July 2008 edition of the White Dragon Oracle

For years I have tried to cultivate a deeper understanding of humankind by studying the ways in which people express their most profound and fundamental emotions. After nine decades of observation, I am now confident enough to dispense advice and expound the deeper workings of the human heart. I hope you will find these musings helpful.

As we enter through the Gates of Summer, my mind turns fondly toward the warm, sunny days of my youth. Though my childhood was spent in the twilight of imperial China, a turbulent, harrowing time for many, I remember only the good times, the small happy moments. I had no idea my family's fortune had vanished. Nor did I know that from one day to the next my parents scraped and scrounged for enough food to stave off the gaunt specter of famine from the door of our once grand home. As a child, I knew only that mother and father loved my brother, sister, and I. Our poor circumstances were not realized until I was much older. As a tot, I felt as if my life was only gold and jade.

Children seem to take in stride, that measure of sorrow we must all bear in this life. In their hearts there is always the hope that life will be better and their days will be happy. No child endures a Winter day without dreaming of Spring. So let us be as children. When troubles fall like the leaves in Autumn and cover us over, let us dream as children do of the coming Spring when the rivers of freshly fallen rain will wash away the accumulated decay and leave only the green grass and newly sprung flowers.

Be Thankful

The spirit of Thanksgiving seems simple enough; to be thankful not that your needs have been supplied, but also that your wants have been met. And how many of us do not have the necessities of life in abundance? Still we have a hard time being thankful, truly thankful. I know I struggle with this issue.

I am still healthy at my advanced age, I have not yet entered my dotage, and I have all that is required to keep body and soul together. Yet, as the Christian bible says, it is the little foxes that spoil the vine. I can not count the times that I looked at the wasp and missed seeing the flower it was lit upon. How many glorious sunny days have passed by as my mind was busy with a million piddling thoughts? I can not even imagine all the joys I have missed by being focused on the 'little foxes' that daily enter my life.

This is not a lesson that can be learned once. You must labor daily to keep worries, those monsters of the mundane, at bay. I was in my teens when I first understood that my cares for the petty and vane world were stealing away happy moments. I sat in my room fussing over a little jade comb with a peony design. My sister had dropped candle wax on it. I was angrily picking the wax that had embedded itself in the intricate design on the comb and in between its finely-fashioned teeth. My cheeks were crimson and my eyes were hot with tears. Suddenly through the latticed window I heard laughter in the courtyard. My mother had emerged from her garden and was giving my sister and two of my young cousins a lesson on the proper way to catch a butterfly. I listened intently to my mother's voice and the mirth that filled the air when my cousins and sister sang a little chant encouraging each other in their pursuit of a rather grand butterfly with blue and black wings.

    I realized that I was missing out all because of a few drops of wax on a jade comb. Still, my pride would not let me rise from my chair. Oh, even now I can't help but urge my younger self to go out and join them.

    Finally my mother came into my room and begged a pitcher of cold water to give a drink to my sister and cousins. I gave her the pitcher and three little bamboo cups. She left and gave my sister and cousins a drink and then fanned them while they rested in the shade. I put my comb aside and wept -- not because of any injustice wrought upon me by another, but for a wrong that I had done myself. Instead of sitting in the shade on a hot day, thankful for the joy and entertainment brought about by a frolic with my dear ones, I sat mourning for flowers that were left ungathered. Sadly that was not the only time when I remembered too late, to shoo away those little foxes.

    Let us, this day, be thankful for all the little things. Fill your heart with the simple joys of life and there will be no room for the trifles that so easily beset us all. If we spend even one day in the thankless twilight of petty thoughts, we will have missed the gratitude brought about by a thousand songs, a thousand laughs, and ten thousand flowers blooming around us.

Thoughts on Being 100 Years Old

What can one say about being one hundred years old? Well, I surely do not feel that old. In my heart I am still a young maid and my soul overflows with wonder and with the desire to soar with cranes and to leap through the autumn hills with the deer. To one's eternal spirit a century is no more than a moment, a blink of the eye.

The body is another thing entirely. It isn't the weight of the flesh as it settles and ages; that isn't too much to bear. Wrinkles and stiff joints are troublesome, but those ailments and other failings do not age the soul either. To the contrary, white hairs bring glory to an aged head. There is honor, bestowed by heaven, for those who have walked this mortal path for ten thousand miles and there is great respect from the young for those stooped and transformed by many years. A person who carries well a long life and is full of joyous days inspires awe in all, for they have endured-- warriors favored by heaven, fighting, nay, defying the pull of the yawning, hungry grave. Yet, there are those who reach an advanced age that are not worthy, for those the crown of many years means nothing. Their glory will be as a tattered garment instead of a gold-thread robe.

What then ages a soul? Loss in all its varied forms can bring one low. Fear with its heavy hand it grabs, claws, and if one allows, paralyzes its victims. Those things are poisonous, but one thing is yet worse: dissatisfaction! This evil will not only rob you of your joy and halt the fruition of your happiness; it will destroy family bonds, community, and brotherhood. Forget not also, that dissatisfaction consumes youth and vitality. Those that give in to this beast are not long for this earth. Many discontented souls have passed early through the gates of the grave. So, let not yourself covet that which is not yours, nor reach the treasures of this earth which lie beyond your grasp! Instead, cultivate in your heart peace and joy and heaven will bestow upon your head many years and you will lay yourself to rest with a satisfied mind.

Sweet Memories

When one is old and knows that the twilight of life has fallen, memories of the past seem to appear more often than guests of flesh and blood. A scent, a sound, an old photo, a word spoken aloud-- any or all of those things might evoke a nearly forgotten moment and suddenly you find an old familiar face, a stolen moment, a soft peal of laughter echoing from some golden afternoon.

Today, for instance, as I sat copying holy texts, I had the urge to lay down my brush and put my paper aside and find a hairpin that my mother had given me on the eve of my wedding. I called for my grand nephew Yan to carry down my bridal chest from the attic.

As he set the tattered old box down, a million thoughts raced through my mind. The faded paintings of butterflies and blossoms brought a smile to my face. But that was nothing compared to what happened when I opened the box. The scent of the past drifted upward to my nostrils. The fragrance of ten thousand days wafted upward from the light pink silk that covered the items in the box. I was instantly transported back to my childhood home-- to the small, but tidy, room that my sister and I shared. Unbelievably green bamboo, dappled with sunlight, was waving in a slight breeze just outside the open window. The pulled-back pink gauze curtains let in the scent of wild roses, and song birds and insects lulled us into an early summer, mid-day drowse with their varied melodies.

My sister was younger and than I. She was intelligent and dutiful, and never quite knew how wonderful she made our lives. I recall her, that particular day, placing items in the new bridal chest that my brother had brought me from Peking. I was marrying into a family of scholarly renown, and only the best would do. She laughed as she looked at the items and teased me gently, as was her way.

From the outer courtyard I heard my mother's voice, "Daughters, our head gardener says the peaches are coming along nicely this year. Your father went to the orchards to see for himself. Are you two asleep?"

She peeped through the diaphanous curtain that hung over the door.

"Still messing with that box!? Ah?" she chided. "You will break some of the delicate items if you are not careful."

"I'm always careful." my sister said, as she stepped from the bed, leaving the small, but exquisite box and its contents alone.

"Go on, now." she said to my sister. "See to your grandma. She is fussing on cook and needs to be calmed down. Take her a fan and ask for a story." My mother knew that nothing pleased her mother-in-law, like being asked about the olden days when the family had great honor bestowed upon them by the imperial court. Those days were gone, but in my grandmother's dreams, they lingered on. Just as now, my golden days, linger on only in the dreams of this silly old woman.

My sister retrieved a pretty hand fan painted with peonies and court ladies and danced off toward the main hall of the house. My mother sat down next to me and gently took a bundle from the folds of her sleeve. She slowly removed the pale blue silk that covered the object, until at last, it was revealed to be a finely carved hairpin made of jade, perfectly white and flawless. With her small, delicate fingers she traced out the design of a dragon and phoenix amongst clouds.

"See how finely this is carved?" she placed it carefully into my eager hands. "It was my mother's hairpin, and her mother's before her. It was all that was given me by her when I left home. I treasure it, for it is all I have of her. Likewise, there will be a day when all you have of me is this hairpin and the few memories that the years will allow you to keep. When you hold it, think of me. And no matter where my ghost is, I will be at peace."

"I will." I said as I pondered the finely etched design.

I was deeply touched, but at the time, my heart was young and I did not fully understand how beloved that item would become. It was only with many years and much loss that I truly understood how precious the hairpin is. Yes, it is merely a piece of carved stone, an excellent example of craftsmanship, a treasure, yet, it is still without flesh and bone and without breath-- a stone. The reason it means so much to me is that it is a tangible item that is mystically connected to an intangible moment. In its fine lines, are the lines of my mother's face, in its smoothness, is the smoothness of her hair, and in its chime, is the chime of her laughter. All the tiny details of that day are recorded in its molecules. Not just that day, but a thousand days, a thousand joys, a thousand tears, and endless songs sang in scented, distant chambers.

     Yan, every helpful, found the hairpin and gave it to me. Though nearly 80 years had passed since that day, once my frail, withered hands touched it, I was there again. Tears came to my eyes and my heart beat fast as sweet specters came to comfort me. Yan asked if he should put away the hairpin and take the chest away. The young never understand the foolish tears of the old. When you are young, you cry in sadness for things you can not obtain. When you are old, you weep tears of joy for things that you did obtain, but could not hold on to. No matter how strong the hands, they can not hold time, love, or fading dreams.

Change

You can no sooner stop change from occurring in your life than a cloud can resist the winds that pull it along. The present is all you have, the future is a dream, and clinging to the past is as futile as a bloom clinging to the bough, when it's time has passed. Only when the bloom has fallen, can the fruit grow and come to fruition. Don't cower in the shadow of change. Embrace it with faith and with hope walk forward into tomorrow. Life is not many days, but one moment, that moment you are experiencing now. To carry all the days you have lived with you, will only burden you and rob you of the present.

Lift up your head from the pillow on which you weep and live, fearless and boldly. There will be time enough to rest when flowers fade and the dust calls your name.

The Nine Joys of Being Old

People erroneously assume there are no good points to being aged. This is a foolish assumption.

1. To be free from convention.
   The rules of the world seem to matter little at my advanced age. If I do not bow or forget to extend a certain courtesy, it is quickly forgiven and marked up to my dotage.

2. To be invisible.
   When you are elderly, you are a ghost among men. On the streets and at home you are ignored. Free from scrutiny, you are left to haunt the pages of books or soak in a pretty day with no one there to disturb you.

3. Your words are considered wise.
   Not all people of advanced years are wise. Still, when a withered hand is raised and words emanate from a head crowned with silver hair, no matter how foolish the words, they are deemed sagacious. Still, as it has been for endless generations, the young rarely follow the advice of their elders. Alas, elders rarely follow their own advice. All men are determined to make the same mistakes, taking all the wrong turns along life's path, and that is as it should be.

4. One is not obliged to attend tedious gatherings.
    For most of my life I attended each family gathering, each wedding, each funeral, and any of a multitude of events that robbed me of time and gifts. If I did not appear, I lost respect and favor. Now, I can casually dismiss the most important invitation, and I am thought of nonetheless for my unwillingness to comply. In fact, many times I am sure it is a relief to the host that I have declined.

5. It is no longer important to guard your words.
    The greatest freedom of age is the freedom to speak your mind. No one will dare to contradict you. They will smile, nod, swallow their indignation and go their way.

6. Vanity fades.
    Of course one always likes to look their best, but as you age you begin to understand that beauty comes from within. In fact there is no other place for it to come from. The beauty of the old comes from a happy smile and a youthful heart. If one does not possess those treasures, you will be thought of as hateful and ugly.

7. Death loses its power.
    There is always a certain sorrow in thinking of departing this world, no matter how many years you live. Still, when one as lived a life full of many joys and many experiences, and the flesh has seen its better days, the thought of perpetual rest gains a certain appeal. There is also the fact that in the final mile of life you have more loved ones on the other side of the veil, than on you do on this side. It only makes sense to go to meet them in the splendid Autumn Hills than

to make such a multitude travel back to this dusty plain of existence.

8. Understanding.
	Through struggles and trials, the soul is purified and the mind is enlightened. As long as one retains their lucidity, they are a walking encyclopedia of dos and don'ts, advice for all occasions, humorous anecdotes, and home remedies to cure a cold or to mend a broken heart. If one is still foolish when quite old, there really is no hope and no excuse for such folly.

9. Appreciating all things.
	Once a person learns that each day, each moment, each joy, each nourishing meal is a blessing that not all possess, then one truly appreciates all things. Life is a great treasure and each moment, each step upon the path, takes us toward a great unknown land in which all things will become clear. So appreciate your moments of sadness and doubt as much as you appreciate your joys and moments of mirth.

Cherish

    Pure love is a simple thing. It isn't a willful action as much as a compulsion. Humans were meant to seek out beauty in all of its forms and cherish it.

    For instance, it is easy to love a flower. A flower is elegant and gives only joy, and we know, all too well, that it will soon fade away. So, we take extra care to inhale its fragrance, to trace the lines of its petals, to sit it in a place of honor and to point it out to all that come by. How much more so should this apply to the people love?

    When you have a loved one, neglect them not, for all too soon, just as a fragile blossom, they too will fade. Take your dear ones-- be it children, a spouse, a parent, or friend-- and exalt them above all other treasures. More rare than gold, finer than jade is one that is beloved. Sit them apart and make them feel special. Point out their best aspects to all that pass by. Trace the lines of their face and store them in your heart, commit them to memory. Note their voice and their laugh....these will be sweet perfume and a balm for the soul in years to come.

    Cherish, my children. Cherish. That is the surest way to know that you love aright.

Romantic Love

    Oh dear, dare a woman of five score years tackle such a subject. Perhaps, I am the best person to comment upon the gentle war that is romance. When one is embroiled in the battle one can not clearly see the battlefield. I, however, stand upon a distant precipice and can see all the landmarks, all the pitfalls, all the ambushes that are part and parcel of amorous pursuits.

    All romantic love starts as attraction. It is only with time, care, and much sacrifice that you find if the love is true. Only through jubilation and sorrow can two souls grow to be true companions. It isn't instantaneous (or if it is, it is only on rare occasions). Sadly, many married couples never become close companions. It was even rarer in the days of my youth. For at that time, there was rarely a choice on which one was to wed. It was a question of politics, prestige, or even something as unromantic as business deal. Women were rarely considered more than chattel to their father and sometimes less than chattel to their husbands. Nowadays, things are easier and there is a choice in who one can wed, yet there are still so many people that believe they are in love, but love amiss, and end up in dismal unions with people they do not respect, nor love. Such arrangements can end in nothing but regret and resentment. That is no way to live a life. It is better to be dead than to live in a house with no peace with someone who is not your equal.

I was lucky. Though my marriage was arranged, my parents did care and picked a man they felt would compliment my personality. My father, whom I never truly knew, longed for happy grandchildren. He knew that children could not be happy in a home wherein dwelt not love. So he took that into account when making the selection. My husband was handsome and studious and from a fine, old family. Our attraction to each other grew as we matured. By the time he departed, we were one. He knew my heart as well as I knew his. And when he ascended to the ancestors, a part of me went with him. You can not love one so wholly and not die a little bit when they fade from this life. That is why when you are old, and used to parting with dear ones, you are, in fact, more ghost than human-- so little of your soul remains.

So, choose well when you seek romance. Find someone that will be your equal, not your better, nor someone that you will constantly condescend to. Let it be someone that stands upon the same ground you stand upon. Well.....I'll say no more about choosing a partner in life. Why? If you are wise you will listen to your heart. Your heart will not lead you astray. If you are foolish, then no words from a fading shadow can help.

A Simple Meal

A simple meal is the best. Humans are greedy and, if given the chance, can become very finicky and unappreciative in any facet of life. This is especially true when pertaining to diet. Giving in to your desire for grand banquets of sumptuous treats and decadent sweets will not serve your body well at all. It will degrade the inner workings and slow the mind. Show me a glutton and I will show you a dullard and a sluggard.

Think of it this way; an engine needs only fuel to move its parts, and oil to lubricate its joints. Anything else, any impurities and it will become inefficient and eventually grind to a halt. The body is such a machine. I have always practiced moderation in my diet, and only rarely drank or ate to excess. It has served me well. I am now over one hundred and I have few of the ailments that plague people that are half my age.

Junk food has its appeal, but you must remember the harm it will do to you. A simple meal is best, just as a simple melody is the sweetest and a simple solution the most practical.

Peace of Mind

      Should someone offer me a great kingdom and all the riches that lay therein, or peace of mind. I would choose the latter. For wealth and prestige can not console a troubled spirit, nor can it dull a conscience that is a aflame with guilt or regret.

Suicide

In the classic novels I read as a young lady, and in many of the folktales recounted to me by my elders, suicide was given a romantic twist. Of course not every instant of depriving oneself of life was considered good or worthy, but if done correctly, nothing could be nobler than ending one's life; for honor of self or your family, for duty to your job or your emperor, or for love. It is considered the greatest sacrifice one can make.

I say that, so that you, gentle friend, will be able to see where I am coming from as I speak on this subject. Though I know it is not good to take one's own life, I still have remnants of those tales of beautiful death in my mind. Fiction is far removed from reality. Let me relate to you one instance in my own life that changed my view of suicide and shattered the sweet orb that I had encapsulated this sorrowful act.

It was early in what the West calls the Warlord Era in Chinese history. We called it life-- an endless road of hardship along which only handfuls of peace could be gleaned. It was in the tumultuous time that a cousin of mine became entangled with a gang of well-intended thugs called the Seven Tigers of Peach Fragrance Street (that was the street upon which our family compound bordered-- it seems a bit too poetic for a gang's name in English, but that was the name). These young men allied themselves with a certain local political leader, a radical young man with a polluted mind who called himself, Little Captain. He in turn was connected to a general, equally corrupt, who was thusly connected to one of the warlords that controlled most of the province and vied for power, along with others, for the heart of the whole empire. Soon, the warlord they had pledged their lives to, was disposed and imprisoned by a new warlord. Thereafter all of cronies were rounded up and soundly interrogated. One thing lead to another and the political leader from our city, the hero of the Seven Tigers, was cast into jail. He had been such a vehement supporter of the has-been warlord, that the new seat of power feared he may well fan the flames of discontentment into a raging inferno.

Daily Little Captain sent notes to the Seven Tigers and urged them to rise up and free him from his cell. He wanted them to bribe officials, or if need be, commit murder. These requests, pleas, and demands took their toll on the youths. They had neither the will to rise up or to kill, nor the money to bribe the jailers to release Little Captain.

I am not sure which one of the Seven Tigers suggested the plan, but inspired by a tale from antiquity, he cajoled the others into joining into a pact with him: if the leader was not freed, they would fast; if he was killed for his cause, they would, in turn, kill themselves and ascend to heaven with their beloved Little Captain.

Sure enough, Little Captain was killed while in jail only days later. Not until much time had passed did we learn that he died after assaulting another prisoner -- a most undignified tale that I will abstain from recounting. The Seven Tigers knew only that their hero, at the hands of brutes, had fallen into the oblivion of glory. They took the body, once it had been unceremoniously expunged from the jail and sat vigil around his body, weeping and bemoaning his passing. Many think women the sillier of the sexes, but young men, with their passions inflamed, are truly the silliest of all creatures under Heaven. When they had wept until their tears refused to flow, they gathered their resolve and swallowed poison. Seven young men, none older than twenty and one, perished in only a matter of minutes.

    Let me describe the scene as they imagined it: Seven proud, loyal soldiers, taking their own lives for the honor of their family, for the glory of the fallen Little Captain, who lay before them on an alter, swathed not in just grave clothes, but majesty and righteousness, and for their noble ancestors, who demanded nothing less than complete, blind devotion to the lofty ideals of the ancients. One by one, the poison tablets were swallowed, and one by one the tigers closed their eyes softly and fell into a peaceful slumber. From that sleep their souls ascended to the heavenly court. There, being found virtuous, they were carried upward into the realm of the immortals-- brothers bound by an oath and by love, sitting in the exalted palaces of honor along side all of the great warriors of the past.

    What my father saw when he found them in their secret meeting place: The deteriorated body of Little Captain lying on platform of fruit crates, wrapped in the bloody, filthy sheet he had been tossed out of prison in. Round about the dispatched troublemaker, there laid the bodies of seven boys, not tigers, but boys. They were not enshrined in marble or in peaceful repose, but they lay entombed in squalid filth and evacuated excrement. They lay, contorted into horrid positions from their death throws, with their faces fixed, wide-eyed and slack-jawed as they faced the consequences of the final deed: death, inglorious and undignified.

They died not for a just cause, but in pursuit of the cause of fools. There was no honor in this death. No great wail went up when the news of their death was reported. Hardly anyone beyond the border of Peach Fragrance Street marked the passing of the Seven Tigers. Even then it was not the jubilant passing of heroes into immortality, but wasted youth into cold, horrid graves. There are times in ones life when events demand the sacrifice of your life to save the lives of others. Such a sacrifice isn't planned it merely happens in a moment. A hero acts and does not think of the glory.

From then on the tales of yore seemed to lose a bit of their gilding. Knowing the truth had dulled my childish dreams.

Truly, most suicides are not for noble reasons, but for selfish ones. We are ungrateful for life and cower at the thought of going forward, so we wish for death and dream of how sad everyone would be at our passing. We conceitedly ponder the depths of mourning our loved ones would be thrown into. We contemplate how the world will shiver and refuse to turn once we have left. Foolishness! It is a sin to bring such anguish to your loved ones and friends, and as for the rest of the world…..does a mountain mourn over the loss of a grain of sand or the sea over one drop of water? Live your life, fear not the future, and know that your time is short enough without being trimmed shorter. No matter the sorrow, our suffering if earthly and not eternal. Take it from one so close to death: live!

The Power of Affection

I know the affection shared by a couple in love is very special, but when one loves wholly, be it a spouse, a child, a parent, or friend, the heart is ever on the line. When a loved one speaks they can raise you up from the grave of sorrow with one gentle word. They can build in your heart an empire of joy in a moment. Conversely, with one slight, one harsh statement, they can raze those ivory towers and lay waste to endless fields of blooms. With the wag of a finger one's heart can be cut into a thousand pieces.

Therefore, I urge all of you, my gentle friends, to guard your words when speaking to loved ones. Know that one kind gesture from you can make a rainbow in their sky or bring rain to the barren fields of their soul. Be gentle, for there will be a time when your heart aches and you will long for someone to comfort you.

Lastly, never turn away true love and affection. It is too hard to gather up once it has been shattered. Never return anger for devotion and never take too lightly the fragility of another's heart. The Creator gave us all the ability to love, but also the ability to hate. Each one of these emotions must be used wisely and never carelessly. Both bear with them great responsibility and hardship and things must be sacrificed for each. Remember though, only love bears joyful fruits. Hate and coldness of heart, brings only the bitter fruits of loneliness.

Thoughts on God

      I was raised as Buddhist and Taoist. I studied Confucianism extensively as a young adult, and after arriving in the United States, I dedicated several years to educating myself in the Holy Bible and the Koran. I do not in any way consider myself an expert on any matter of faith. I am no theologian. I am merely a lowly woman whose soul hungers for knowledge and understanding.

  The more I read and studied the more I saw that life is not merely a world of black and white. There are very few constant rights and absolute wrongs. The greater portion of life and morality is a vast and varied palate of gray. There is a human morality, something innate -- the spirit of God, the spirit of the Creator, and a common collective knowledge of what is wrong and what is right. Then there is the morality of men: rules, laws, and conventions that attempt to order a society, but usually only manage to burden it and stifle it from any sort of inner growth.

  By saying that, I am not railing against any religion or anyone's faith in a deity or particular set of morals. I am saying though, that no religion, nothing formulated by man, can bring one closer to God (whatever form you choose to see Him in). Each person must look within and seek the truth that the Creator instilled in us all. A holy book can guide you and instruct you, and in times of need there can be solace gleaned from the words of righteous men and women, but unless you are willing to seek a truth beyond the canon and scriptures, then you will never fully realize God.

   I sat many a day and wished I could see some great sign; some grandiose vision that would assure me my faith has not been wrongly placed. But no such sign came. It was only the quiet moments, when my heart was still and my mind uncluttered that I could hear the small, hushed voice of the Creator. It was in those moments that I knew my faith was justified.

We should not know the Creator too well. If we knew his plans, if we knew what steps he was about to take, we would only falter in the pathway and become stumbling blocks in the grand scheme. We are fallible. The Creator is not. We see and care for the finite. The Creator sees all and knows the infinite.

A Discourse on the Christian Bible

　　I have waded through the lengthy tomes of Chinese classics both in my youth and again when my understanding was keener, but never have I encountered such a ponderously enigmatic book as the Christian Bible. Perhaps it is because I view it from the eyes of an Easterner, and do not fully grasp the delicate nuances of the language and the context of it within a culture different than my own. Still, if you will suffer me to do so, I would like to give a few thoughts I had on this Holy Text.

　　I have heard teachers and ministers alike discuss the Bible. Some were learned with years of formal education and others were, as they say, led by the Spirit. In my opinion it is best if there are both forces at work. When a book is so old and covering such a vast and complex time span, it is important to know the historical and social context in which it was written. Without such context and proper interpretation it is likely that many errors and problems will arise when trying to apply its principles to day to day life.

　　I feel, after years of study (not only of the Bible itself, but commentary by saints, scholars, critics, and sagacious historians) that the Old Testament is a grand history of a people and their struggle to overcome their own failings and the hardships of building a nation. There are insights into the human condition, wise sayings, comforting passages, and beautiful psalms, but as the New Testament teaches, it is all in all a witness and not a guide on how to live righteously. It would be to difficult to live by the rules of a wandering, desert people, who as it is shown, could not live up to their end of the covenant with God. Many say I am wicked to dismiss any of the texts as only history or texts of comfort. I remind them though, that the Bible (despite the erroneous beliefs of many) is not The Word of God. Christ is the Word and only Christ and his words should be revered, not merely the written texts.

      Now to the New Testament-- this is a book I can relate to. The Gospels of Christ are some of my favorite reading. I am awed by the love, the sacrifice, and the great message of hope and unification that is taught by Jesus. All too often I feel that Christians forget the simple, pure message of their Savior. They neglect the two greatest commandments of Christ: Love God above all and love your neighbor as yourself. Truly if one practiced these two principles, the world would be a different place. As with any faith, it is only a living religion when the practitioners live their faith daily. If one claims to be a Christian, a Buddhist, a Muslim, or any other faith, and does not practice it, then they are truly sinful and poor ambassadors of their Deity. If someone was ill it would be better to admit that you are not a doctor, than to say you are and cause them further harm or even death. How much more important is it to not lead the soul of another to ruin. A body returns to the dust, the soul returns to God.

Let me get back on course for my final thoughts on the Bible.

I have gathered many handfuls of spiritual nourishment from this tome. By reading and applying the tenets of the faith, I have become a disciple of Christ. This is in no way contrary to the principles I was taught as a child. I want only to love those that society has cast out. I want to be the angel that feeds the weary, or the pilgrim that carries the load of some tired soul, so that they might not faint on this arduous journey of life. If you are in need of hope and in need of some gentle hand to point the way, read the first four books of the New Testament. Take to heart the words of Christ. Then when you are confronted by an unchristian Christian you can politely give them instruction and guide them back on course.

What Is Right?

It seems that in these modern days people are forever asking, "What is right? What is wrong?" Perhaps there is no single answer. Perhaps morality can only be defined within the bounds of a society, a faith, or a certain culture. Perhaps, but I think not. To me there is a universal morality that transcends religion, time, society, and culture. There is a basic set of commands, you might say, that can be applied to any one of any time, any place, no matter the political or religious persuasion. They are as follows:

1. Honor life in all of its forms.
2. Respect each other, without exception.
3. Accept personal responsibility for your actions.
4. Always be quick to forgive and slow to anger.
5. Rob no one of their dignity lest yours be taken away.
6. Remove yourself from any hurtful or negative influence.

All other mores can be extrapolated from these five commandments. Consider carefully how your actions will affect others and how their actions affect you. Act accordingly and do all things with love and respect and you will always be justified.

Contemplating a Portrait of Kwan Yin

Written in a museum, while looking at a Ming Dynasty scroll painting (June 21, 1989):

Clothed in white and blue, you are the epitome of goodness. With the silvery moon as your crown, and the stars as your palace, you ride through the celestial kingdom upon an ancient dragon.

How many times I have longed to be as you, above reproach and ever benevolent, yet, I have failed! Have I wasted my days in vain pursuits? Have I fretted away my hours with worries of this temporal world? Yes. I have. All along my heart should have been set upon eternal things and my hands hard at work comforting the sick and poor.

I know not what hand held the brush that painted you upon this piece of silk, so long ago, but surely it was a hand guided by Heaven. A painter of worth and virtue, for who else would dare draw the form of one so magnanimous and exalted, except one anointed by Heaven? Perhaps no human hand did this work, but some immortal artist. Perhaps it was you, with divine ink and with stardust that cast this image from nothingness? Surely, that must be so, for I know I look upon the face of a deity, Mercy incarnate.

While I stand here, an unworthy disciple, speak to me, that I might hear your commands and after hearing, might I do those same things you ask of me. What do you say, ancient teacher?

Reproach none.
Judge no one's actions, but your own.
Reap only what you have sown.
Show mercy without bound.
Love unconditionally.
Tell others of these tenets, but be not weary, nor forceful if they resist goodness.

Give me strength that I might do these things and live what days I have left as an adherent to your holy call.

Thoughts Recorded After Attending a Holy Ghost Revival

My dear children, in the process of reading this book you may well have noticed that I mention Christianity quite often. In fact, I reference it more than do the religions/philosophies that were with me since birth. I do this not because I am an authority on the gospels, nor an evangelist for the Christ. I speak of it so often because the homegrown rural sects intrigue me to no end. For the last fifteen years I have lived in a Baptist-centric community in a small town in the rural southeast of the United States. From the first day I arrived I felt the presence of God's lambs. Before the movers had even half-finished their job, a group of women from the neighborhood chapel arrived to welcome with kind smiles, some dishes of food, and some groceries. This seemed a rather large welcome for a stranger, but better fitted to the return of an old friend. Yet, my great nephew Yan's friend, a local boy, assured me this was the usual and in no way obliged me to attend their services. This came as a great relief to me. I had overcome my fear of Catholics (which I acquired as a child, fearful, as many were, that the Jesuit missionaries were going to destroy our culture and our traditions), but had still not quite overcome my reservations about evangelicals and fundamentalists. Many of my friends in the city had warned me of raucous church services in which snakes were bandied about, people shrieked and rolled about on the floor while others ran the aisles and healed people by striking them.

Despite that, I decided that I must attend a service. I knew I had been mistaken about Catholics, and I felt it was needful for me to extend the benefit of the doubt to my new neighbors. Also, I often instruct others that biased thoughts are not conducive to enlightening the mind. So, to keep my credibility, I tossed away my preconceptions and made plans to attend one of the services in the area.

Once I had gathered up the courage and the energy, I, along with Yan and his young friend, went to the first night of what the locals called a Holy Ghost revival meeting at the chapel just down the road from my hermitage. The faithful had named the chapel "Beauty for Ashes." What a poetic name and what a profound meaning. I recalled instantly the passage from the Bible.

To appoint unto them that mourn in Zion, to give unto them BEAUTY FOR ASHES, the oil of joy for mourning, the garment of praise for the spirit of heaviness; that they might be called trees of righteousness, the planting of the LORD, that he might be glorified.-- Isaiah 61:3

As I approached the humble, white washed building, with its doors standing wide open, I felt a sense of peace. The people, especially at the time, due to the isolation of the community had rarely seen someone such as me-- a withered, Chinese flower, with petals of faded silk and ornaments of ancient jade-- yet they welcomed me with much kindness.

My spirit was lifted as the music began. The old upright piano jangled and dinged as the congregation jubilantly sang hymns. It was much louder and less formal than the hymns I had heard at the Catholic services I attended. There was a lot of swaying of bodies and waving of hands. It was very moving to hear so many voices lifted in earnest praise of their God.

After much singing and testimonials, the reverend took the stage. When he loosened his tie and flung his jacket onto a chair, I knew we were in for something, but I had no idea what. The reverend read the scriptures with great authority and then, with a booming voice elaborated on what he had read, quoting other passages by heart and tossing out thoughts left and right. All along, the congregation rang out with "amen" and "praise the Lord!" I was informed later that when everyone was moving and clapping they were in the Spirit. It meant that God had descended and was there with them. I have to admit, I felt a chill, and exhilaration. I was dazzled and somewhat discombobulated, yet I enjoyed myself thoroughly.

I can't say that is my preferred way of being instructed by the anointed teacher, nor do I think all their beliefs are based in the words of Christ, but I have to avow and aver, that those people were sincere in their devotion and praise and they were, in all earnest, worshipping in the best and most proper way they knew.

As soon as I got home, I wrote down my thoughts and observations.

1. To these people God is not a distant, unconcerned deity, he is the father of the universe and he dwells among them, having interest in all facets of their life. He sits enthroned with both the hand of compassion and the sword of vengeance exposed at all times. There is an awesome respect and a terrible fear in these people.

2. There is seemingly neither ritual nor ceremony. It is basically a religious free-for-all. Anyone who wants to sing can sing, anyone who wishes to speak can speak, and should anyone feel the urge to shout, or stand with hands raised, they are permitted and even encouraged to do so.

3. Neither the quality of the voice, nor the ability of the singer matters. Each person who opens their mouth and empties their lungs in praise is lauded and commended for their efforts.

4. An anointed preacher must be young enough to bear the rigors of being in the Spirit. Yet he must be not too young that he will be easily tempted to sin. At the same time, he must not be immature in the faith, or unable to quote scripture. Formal education on the scriptures is not required and sometimes frowned upon. A preacher should read his Bible only and receive his message directly from God and not from the flawed commentary of men, no matter how scholarly and learned they might be.

5. Outsiders are welcome, yet I believe they may

easily become targets. Not out of hate, but out of love and fear for their souls. To be perceived as one that is lost, is a terrible thing to these people and some will go to any means to reunite you spiritually with Christ.

6. They speak often of the End Times when Christ will return and the Earth and all of its unholy inhabitants shall be razed from existence. Some even seem jubilant at the thought of this rapture. I can understand the joy one would feel at being at one with the Creator, yet, I feel that joy must be tempered with sadness at the loss of so many souls.

Over the years I have attended services from time to time, especially on special days. I am always made welcome and have never been harassed. Yet, I know to them I believe amiss and I am lost and lacking a relationship with God. This does not bother me, because I think they have, in certain areas, believed amiss and have a skewed perception of the Creator, the father of all mankind. These differences in opinion though, do not keep me from helping them when they are not in need, nor does it keep them from coming to my aid. They are merely pilgrims in a strange land, just as I am, trying to find their way back to the birthplace of the soul. They are as sincere as the most devout Buddhist monk and as human and in need of grace and mercy as the poorest, most abhorred drunk lying in a filthy gutter.

I will keep learning of their ways and do my best to enlighten them to my truth as reverently as they wish to enlighten me to their truth. When I am narrow-minded and hardhearted, I pray they will be gentle with me and love me still, just as I will do when they resist reason or cling to some false notion. I believe a possible reason for so many religions, sects, and denominations is because God wants it that way. He made us all different. It is easy to oppose or hate someone that is different; it is nature to do so. So, if we can love each other despite our differences, then we have overcome nature and we have touched the divine. We will never be the true children of mercy, until we can extend our love to all people, no matter their lifestyle, faith, or persuasion.

Ponderings for the New Year

As I sit here at my desk, head resting upon my hand, contemplating the New Year ahead and the current year which will soon depart, my mind is whirling with both regret and hope. I will address the regret first, so that I might end on a happy note.

Regret:
      When you are a child, a teen, and even a young adult, you will do things that you regret at the time. These are small things that tear the heart for a moment, but in the grand landscape of life they are but tiny trees on some distant slope. It is not until one is old, until a thousand frosts makes white your hair and the weight of ten thousand days stoops your shoulders toward the earth, that one truly understands regret. That kind of regret can paralyze one and rob them of the will to live. That type of regret is hard to battle. I have warred with such regrets for years. I use my faith, my inner-peace, and the love of my dear ones to keep this beast at bay. Yet it lurks, ever near, and often roars and thunders its hooves just over the horizon when my mind, especially at this time of year, wanders back through days gone by.

      How can one avoid such regret? The awful

truth is, that no one can avoid regret totally. It is impossible. We are all flesh and blood and prone to mistakes. We all hurt others; we harm ourselves, selfishly turn away others in need, and selflessly ignore our own needs. The time to avoid regrets is when you are young and able. When you are as I, shackled by age and weakened by a failing body, there is no way to turn back and right wrongs and recapture lost opportunities. In such a state, the heart grinds and screams for another chance, but my dears, in this world when age is upon us; there is no second chance to again be youthful and capable. So, while you are young gather your blossoms. If your mother calls your name, answer with joy. If a lover desires your kiss, give it freely. If your faith demands you help another, help them with out hesitation. If your child needs comforting, put aside your work and comfort the small one. If a flower opens before you, inhale its fragrance with vigor. These are the things which make life sweet. Work does not, a life of self-loathing does not, nor does a life of missed opportunities and resentment make for a joyful longevity.

So, my young ones, reach out to the blossom laden bough, and take the blooms in hand and cherish them. To enjoy life, each moment, to cherish each small step of the journey, is the greatest gift from God, and all the heavens and all those that have passed before know it. This brings me to the next topic.

Hope:
Hope is often spoken of, but few people have it. Certainly, all of us say "I hope," as we toss our words around casually, but few of us truly cultivate

hope within out hearts. True hope: the type of hope that can carry you over the cold, lonesome rivers of life. Genuine hope will help you stave off the specters of your regrets and your misdeeds. This pure, divine hope will show you the light at the end of the tunnel. I do not mean to sound trite in that statement. It is the only way; my muddled old mind can express the inexpressible.

The hope of which I speak is the hope of confirmation, the hope of attaining a goal. If life was a meaningless race and the only reward, the embrace of the grave, what hope could one truly ever have? For each action would be meaningless, each deed would be just another step toward oblivion. Perhaps I am foolish for believing in a higher realm of being, but I do. It gives me hope. Hope that my life was not just vanity; hope that my shortcomings will be erased by my good deeds. Hope that the grave will not be my eternal bed, but to live and to be one with the Creator, to bask in the spiritual light of all goodness. Hope that one day despair, regret, and the evils of this flawed world will feel the sting of death, and trouble our souls no more.

Those are my hopes. Those are the wishes of my heart. Those are the things that will help me face the New Year and each new day. Someone told me once, 'hope for the
Old is more precious than gold.' This is a truthful statement. I will give you a pound of gold for each ounce of hope you have to give.

Spring

    Summer is for laboring, Autumn is for dreaming, and Winter is for contemplation. Spring, however, is the season for living. Put aside the brush and paper think no more of the classics, defrock yourself of the heavy garments of winter, and don vernal robes in colors as gay and bright as the flowers newly sprung all around.

    Spring is the time to sit beneath the fragrant, snowy boughs of peach and apple trees. While there, drowsy with the intoxicating perfume that they emit, quote poems of love and recite prose of devotion. Let the gentle breeze, still cool and exhilarating; carry you from the bright cheery day to the calm, tranquil evening. Watch, for in that crepuscular light, dreams are flesh and flesh are dreams. Fairies dance upon every hill and dragons drink from the sapphire pools that gather in the clouds at dusk. In such an environment a bird's call could easily be mistaken for the voice of an old friend calling your name. Or is it not a bird's song? Perhaps a distant companion has strayed down some forgotten path to visit you in your seclusion?

    I always go out on such Spring evenings to say my farewell to the sun. Many times as the night falls all around and the chill deepens, I glance, with aged eyes, from the garden pavilion in which I sit, and see the warm glow of the windows that beckon me homeward. For a moment I am a young girl again, coming in from an evening stroll, and I know that soon, my mother will peer from one of the illuminated panes, worried that her eldest daughter will catch a chill.

"Heat the tea for me! I'm on my way, mama." I mutter softly, knowing no one is there to hear me. They are only shades of Spring evenings, now some nine decades past.

Summer

When the weather is hot, and the estival days of year are upon us, I find I remain calm and cool by turning my attention to softer pursuits. I will give you five examples from nature to convince you that this isn't merely the prattling of an ancient woman.

1. The gentle cicada does not spend the long August days flying back and forth in the hot sun. No. He finds a lofty bough where he can catch even the most gentle breeze. Once there he does not toil, but sings his song until the evening sun fades. That is why you will often find me on a high, shaded balcony, singing sad songs and odes of old.

2. The cackling, jolly hen no longer has her brood to tend and often spends the humid hours of a Summer's day scratching characters in the sand near the water's edge where the breeze from the water steals the sting from the air. Being an old hen myself, I often take refuge in my waterside pavilion and use my jade brushes to write poems and copy sutras in my scratchy old calligraphy. However, unlike the hen I do avoid swallowing wasps if at all possible.

3. Horses are a nostalgic folk and make good use of days which are too hot to work. They leave their burdens at the gate, find a comfy patch of grass and think of days gone by, recite odes and dream

of times when they galloped off to war. Not as nimble as a horse, I lean upon my cane, take a chair in the garden and dream of my girlhood and flowers that have long since faded, fragrant grasses that have withered. Yet, memories remain.

4. Oh my friend the industrious spider, she embroiders her web high in the rafters and never sheds drops of perspiration. With silken threads and good cloth, I take the same needle my grandmother used and embroider butterflies, which are also a favorite subject of my sister, the spider.

5. The pious turtle meditates all day in his chamber beneath a garden stone, praying for peaceful days and a thousand year lifespan. So I, too, sit in my stone chapel and pray for peaceful days and ...Well, it seems I have already lingered here a thousand years!

Autumn

Who can understand Autumn better than the aged? For we are in the Autumn of life. Spring is a sweet memory. Summer in all of its glory has passed. Winter, our final companion, is close at hand.

Still, there are delights in ones Autumn days. The fading leaves of faithful trees burn. The last remnants of life glow intensely. Bright colors fueled by all the passion and furor that is left within their weighty boughs and gnarled limbs. A last moment of glory; they fade, and go down to the grave as bare and as poor, as when they arose from the dust.

In Autumn days, flowers yet bloom, from the noble chrysanthemum crowned with the glory of ten thousand years to the humble, white heads of the fleabane daisy, trampled upon by man and beast alike. It is those final flowers, no matter how small, that are the most precious. Those that bloom when decay is on the march are the most worthy of admiration. What are these flowers of honor? An old cherished friend, a sweet memory, grandchildren who have grown into prosperous adults, a night of joyful dreams, a simple meal with loved ones, a content heart...these are the flowers of Autumn.

On Autumn evenings, the kiss of Winter is in each gust of wind. The thought of death is a comfort, an end to days and struggles. No man can return to

Spring in this life and no amount of lamenting will call back the balmy afternoons of golden Summer. So we must step forward and walk the path before us. I for one will blaze brightly-- an ancient maple with colors like the sun. All will glory in my beauty until the final leaf falls...what more can one ask for?

Winter

     As I grew older, Winter seemed to be more of an enemy. Its cold winds chilled my flesh, all the way to the bone; its sharp teeth tore at my skin, and robbed my blood of its heat. When you are ancient, such as me, you do not need a chill that one glass of brandy can not remedy.

     That being said, I do appreciate this longest season of the year. As I sit here by the window in my study, I look out upon my garden all blanketed in white beneath a sky of dull gray. There is a serene, otherworldliness to the scene before me. I open my window and a rush of frigid air greets my face and I flinch just a bit. There is an invigorating freshness in the air. Like a sip of icy water in the depths of a sweltering summer. My eyes sparkle and I am able to bear the wintery torbor.

     I also owe to Winter one of my most enlightening moments. Once while walking from my house to the mailbox. I recall that I had my bright red, padded, brocade jacket and my black hat. I fancied myself a red bird of winter plodding about in the freshly fallen snow. If not for my black, rice-paper parasol, which Cardinal birds rarely carry, the effect would have been complete.

     As I neared the mailbox, I looked out over the cedar trees and pines that line the country lane which winds past my house. Their boughs, ever green, were weighted mightily with their shimmering, icy burden. All around me was silence; no cars, no phones, no other human voices, only the beat of my own heart and the soft patter of snowflakes on the trees and on my parasol. I peered into the infinite gray of the sky and watched as a million snowflakes fell toward the earth-- a vast expanse of nothingness through which they fell-- just as we fall, through time and space, but for a moment. We live from cloud to earth, from cradle to grave, and then we, as all are destined to do, accumulate with those that have traveled the course before us. Seen only as a blurred multitude by those too busy falling to notice us in detail, and then we are forgotten, melted by the sun of Spring and the warm caress of endless ages.

At the time, I barely grasped all that the epiphany had opened unto me. It took much time and pondering before I could make sense of it all. Since the days were cold and the nights colder, I had plenty of time to ruminate and decipher these thoughts. If my epiphany had occurred in Spring or Summer, might I not have forgotten it all too quickly? Might not a passing butterfly or the scent of freshly bloomed honeysuckle taken away my attention from this celestial vision? So I say, blessed are the days Winter and blessed be the long nights of contemplation. For it is in these times of bodily hibernation that we are able to lay aside the tasks that usually settle upon us and the diversions that so easily steal away our time. For a while we can truly think. If we use this time wisely, we will, like a butterfly in Spring, rise from our winter chamber, a new creature, able to fly beyond any boundary.

Ruminations on Holidays

Written as a Christmas address to her fans in the December edition of the White Dragon Oracle

With all my heart I pray that this Christmas and holiday season will be filled with love and joy.

Though I was raised with only the vaguest idea of the Christian celebration (from Jesuit missionaries in my city), after having lived in the US all these years I have grown to appreciate the holiday and the sentiment behind it -- not the commercialization of the holiday, but its essence.

All holy days and days of celebration, especially when the people are prosperous, take on layers of excess and all the trappings of conspicuous consumption. It is true of the Chinese holidays, and holidays around the world. It is our job to strip away those layers, lest poverty come and do it for us, and adore the pure, unadorned naked beauty of the holiday. What is this core of all holidays? It is simply, thankfulness. At Christmas you are thankful for the birth of a savior; at the Lunar New Year you are thankful for another year of life, for prosperity, for health; and on other days you are thankful for your children, your ancestors, those that have carried the torch before us. No matter the holiday, I always celebrate. Not for gifts, for what could an old lady such as I need? I use these days to draw my loved ones near, the few that linger yet. I remember the days gone by, the sweet, enticing memories of holidays past. Then, when the party breaks and the blossoms are scattered, I bow my unworthy, old head and give thanks. I thank God for another day, another chance to laugh; another chance to sip from the goblet of joyfulness, and for whatever wonders that might lie ahead.

    Think of those things when you are gathered with your family and friends. For there will come a time, when you are old and full of days, that only the memories of such times will remain. When you are the only crane left upon the lake, with only your reflection as a companion. At such a time these days will come to revive you, to carry you through, until at last you are joined with the friends and family that have already ascended.

Advice to a Troubled Friend

My dear Madame Li,

    I hope all is well with you. I pray you are as healthy and vibrant as you were when last I visited you.

    I am sad to say that I am not doing well at all. I have recently lost my job and I am now on the last few weeks of my unemployment benefits. I keep putting in applications, but it seems that no one wants me. I am not sure if it is my age, or the fact that my work experience is so limited. Either way, it is very disheartening, to say the least. My husband is holding up well, but anytime I think money is going to be short, I get worried about our mortgage and about the credit card bills.

    Sorry for the shortness of the note, but I would rather stop here than to write more about my present situation. Perhaps by the time you hear from me again, I will have better news.

    Your devoted friend, A.

    After receiving this letter, I had Yan carry tea to my study and I set down to write an immediate response to my downtrodden friend. I hope it does not embarrass my friend, nor make me seem as a braggart, but I want to share the aforementioned reply, incase it might help someone else suffering from similar woes.

Dear A.,

I am thankful to say that I am indeed doing well. Perhaps better than I deserve. It doesn't seem right for someone as young as you to suffer and someone as I old as I to be so spry. Still, I am happy that Heaven has blessed this unworthy old woman.

It does seem that you are in a bit of financial distress. If I had any money, I would gladly pay your bills, but as Saint Peter said in the bible, silver and gold have I none; but such as I have give I thee. And all I have to give is advice.

My family was prosperous for generations, blessed by heaven and patronized by the imperial household. In those times of plenty, my honored and worthy ancestors saw fit to store a portion of their bounty for times of famine and times of want. Also, my forefathers taught their sons that no matter how much wealth one had, it could be taken away in an instant. Prosperity is as mercurial as life itself. However, as the years of plenty came one after another, each succeeding generation became laxer than the previous, until the time of my grandparent's generation. By the time my father's father had entered into manhood, much of the family's fortune had been squandered needlessly by his elder cousins. The family businesses were under the control of careless, greedy fools and family's farmlands, the ones that were not abandoned totally to squatters, were unproductive. The flow of money that came into the family coffers dwindled as the amount going out grew.

By the time my father came of age, things were indeed very lean. Not only had a draught fallen upon the land, but years of corrupt government and conspicuous consumption among all the elites had brought the whole empire to its knees. As the Empress Dowager resisted reality, the plight of the people worsened. It was in this midnight of the empire that my father became a family man. He worked tirelessly to manage the ancestral farmlands that he had inherited. He reined in unruly farming families, dispelled riotous gangs of thieves, and used every technological advance possible to increase the yield. He also practiced the tenets of his forefathers. When a time of surplus came, he saved for times of want. He borrowed as little as possible and allowed no man to be indebted to him.

We had few luxuries, but we had all the comforts of life. Despite the harrowing times of wars and warlords, we remained in a more or less comfortable state. That is until the Great Leap Forward, but that is an entirely different story.

What I am trying to say is, that no matter what the economic or social climate one must live within their means. Nowadays it is easier than ever to get loans, to reach further, and have more. I am not suggestion you deny yourself all comforts, but heavily weigh large purchases. If they are needful things, do not hesitate. But if they are frivolous, then reconsider. Excess now always equates to want at some future time. Though, I have never had a credit card and I am unsure of all that implies. I do think it is a bad idea to purchase trivial items when not only the resources aren't there, but when there will be interest added to the debt. Insanity!

Do not take my chiding words to mean that I don't sympathize with your plight. I do. If you were not so dear to me, then I would not dispense this advice I have had moments in which I squandered my money and my time. Yet, each time I found myself in such a situation I recalled the sound principles that had brought prosperity to my ancestors. Now, I receive only a fixed amount of money each month. I pay my bills, put some away for unforeseen expenses, and then use what is left for buying extras. The memory of lean times keeps me in line. Perhaps these hard times you face now, will remind you at some later date to be more cautious when you are blessed with surplus. Should you never face such times again, perhaps it will serve your children to remember these times.

When you are near again, do drop by and see me in person. Until then I look forward to your letters.

Sincerely,
Your bothersome Aunty Li.

The Subject of Race

Racism is nothing new to me. I was born into a nation wherein race, or race hatred, played a big role. It wasn't just the long standing tensions between us and the other peoples of Asia; it was also the mistrust and hatred that burned brightly between the various minorities within the Chinese empire. We were in essence one people, but a divided people. In the early years of my life, the ire turned from within and focused more on the Japanese and Western powers.

Even at such an early age, I knew that this hatred was wrong. I knew that we were all one people. We are one species of human, all brothers and sisters. I asked my mother why color and culture separated people. I asked her why one people would hate another people without knowing them. Her answer was, fear.

As I matured and understood the world better, I knew that my mother was right. Though, some would argue that it is ignorance not fear. It is true that ignorance is fear's companion, and in some cases an enabler, but usually it occurs after fear has taken hold and used to justify the fear itself. Allow me to elaborate.

Mistrust, usually instilled in a people by their leaders (be it on a tribal or national level), is the seed from which fear grows. This fear separates and destroys. It is the fear of change, the fear of losing control, the fear that another people will dominate you if you do not dominate them first. These baseless fears pit nation against nation, color against color, and religion against religion.

When I came to the United States, I had little knowledge of how race had little knowledge of how deeply racism was imbedded into the nation's psyche. I had imagined that in the great melting pot, all would be equal. However, I was sad to find that the culture of the time was rife with stereotypes and misconceptions. Being Chinese, I was looked upon as a more or less benign, subservient old woman, who probably worked a laundry or hosted at a restaurant. I was never mistaken for an elderly housewife and scholar. Still, I was on the racism peripheral. The greatest contention was between blacks and whites. This was especially true during my decade here.

I was urged against buying a home in a white neighborhood. I was assured that it wasn't because they thought I'd be a bad neighbor, but that it would set a bad precedent. So, I moved into a black neighborhood and opened a bookstore. I was readily accepted by the community and never had any problems. As time passed, the black neighborhood became a Jewish neighborhood and then a neighborhood for predominantly young, white, hip couples. By that time, the most intense racial times were behind us. I was looked upon as the old book lady down the street, not the old Chinese laundress. Once they knew me, there was no reason to fear me, my customs nor ways.

I know there are still many things left to

accomplish in the realm of battling back biases and fear. There is still racism, but racism is not the only head of this monster. Ageism and sexism are also being battled now. Conservatives and Liberals of all different persuasions now rise up against each other, sometimes with no real reason at all, only fear.

Some will chide me for equating the two, but I honestly believe that homophobia is the newest face of this age old fear that has spawned so many types of hate. There are those out there that have painted all homosexuals with one brush. Stereotypes and misinformation abound. Even those that justify their hate as moral verses immoral, does an injustice to their faith and the love which God has shown them.

Someone said to me once that if we were all of one race, all of one faith, and all of one nation, that there would be peace. I quickly lifted my voice in protest. "Nay," said I, "There would then be those that hate those older than they, those that are younger. There would be men that hate women and wise that turn against the insipid. There would be homophobia and political paranoia. Even if we were all of one nation, one faith, one race, one gender, one intelligence, one social class, and one age-- fear and prejudice would still exist, for humans are flawed creatures."

That statement seems harsh, but it is true. One can hope for, but should never expect, a utopian future. People will always hate, but they can not take your dignity. Dignity is a crown given by Heaven and no person can take it away. You can only be robbed of your dignity when you willingly lay it down. I tell you now that you should battle to keep your dignity more so than for gold or any sort of material gain.

An Angel

From the first time I saw the image of an angel, I was enchanted. These images were few and far between in my native county. After moving to the United States, before becoming a recluse in the country, I often took the city bus to a large Catholic church in a quite neighborhood a few miles away. I went there first to meditate in the holy sanctuary (to me a holy place is a holy place no matter the name over the door). My first time there I sat in a pew, near the back, intent on meditation, but before I could begin, I became entranced by what I saw before me. Looking up I beheld a glorious, luminous window. It bore the image of a lithe, ethereal being, fair-haired and winged neither male nor female, standing watch over a small mortal child. It was such a peaceful vision. To be a small woman alone in a large, cold world is scary. But to have a protector, an angel, to guide your steps and dispel evil from your path, that is a comfort.

For many years I longed to know whether or not such a creature stood near to me. I wanted to believe one did, yet, I was never sure. That is until one day when I was walking from the grocery store back to my home. It was a calm, cool autumn day as I left, but on my way back the clouds darkened, the wind picked up and the temperature fell several degrees. I could see and hear a heavy rain inching its way toward me from a block away. I looked around, but there was no storefront in which to take shelter, only the boarded up windows of an abandoned warehouse. Perhaps such a scene does not seem dire to you, but for me, even though I was only in my 80s, a sudden, chilling rain could easily have been my downfall. If you are blessed to live as long as I, you will know all too well, the fragile nature of one's health.

Suddenly from behind I heard the voice of a young man. I turned to see a rather disheveled man of twenty or so, in a black jacket, a black shirt and ripped jeans. There was a hardedge to his appearance, but his eyes were tender and a look of concern was upon his brow.

"Let me help you." He said as he opened a worn umbrella. He held the umbrella over me as we walked, even though he himself was subjected to the cold downpour. He spoke few words in response to my ramblings as we walked. Once we reached my apartment building, he helped me safely up the steps, beneath the awning and then vanished he into the storm. I walked by the abandoned warehouse every evening for two weeks hoping to see him again. And for the rest of my time in the city, I kept my eye on alert for that young man. I never saw him again.

I know it isn't strange to see someone once in a large city and then never see them again. I am not trying to make the argument that he was a heavenly being. On the contrary, I am making the argument that angels are not heavenly beings. An angel is a messenger, a help or guide in a time of need. There are heavenly angels, I'm sure, but the types that appear to us are flesh and blood. Any person that is willing to sacrifice their comfort and time, to minister unto someone in need. Even if it seems a trivial need, such as a kind word, it could be that little bit of food that gives a tired wayfarer the energy to finish the journey.

A Letter from a Friend

A letter from a friend is, more likely than not, the perfect antidote to cure whatever melancholy has beset me. Each day I eagerly await the mail. 'Tis such a simple event, yet it is also one that seems acutely blessed.

I have been extremely fortunate in my life, when it comes to friends who are willing to correspond with me. I have dear ones all over the world that write me regularly to inquire about my health and my current projects. Such inquires make me feel I have purpose and often inspire to trudge forward, no matter how downtrodden I feel.

Receiving and opening a letter is such a comforting ritual. To carefully open an envelope and retrieve from its belly, a handwritten letter; joyous rapture! Even if it is no more than a note, it is a treasure. The act of someone putting pen to paper and recording one's thoughts and feelings is an intensely personal thing. Sharing it with a friend is an act serene in its intimacy and sacred in its pureness.

When I was young, the written word was considered powerful, nay, magical. When a man set his name to a document, it was an oath. It would be considered a bond as enduring as a tablet of jade. Then being literate was a privilege. Nowadays, people are very flippant about such things, and written words seem to have lost their mystique in the eyes of the populace. Computers and mass produced books have all but eradicated the bond between man and ink and paper. But for dreamers-- artists and poets, alike-- words still hold a very dear and special place. The act of using your hand to hold a writing implement, the tracing of each character onto paper, stringing words together like pearls on a silken thread, a finely written letter, an elegantly addressed envelope, a well-placed stamp; these are actions that produce a work of art, not merely a slap-dash note or an ill-written text message. Is nothing sacred in this twilight of humankind?

    If you truly wish to touch the heart of a distant friend, take a moment to write a letter. It needn't be anything fancy, a postcard will do. The only important thing is that you write upon the paper what is written upon your heart.

Thoughts on Calligraphy

I do not consider myself a master calligrapher. I am a poor hand at this most noble of arts, yet, I have lived long enough to discern the wheat from the chaff. I have been privileged to view some of the greatest works of all time. I hope you will allow an uneducated novice such as me ramble for a few moments on this subject.

Before I set down my list, I must say that it is my belief that one can better judge a man by his hand at calligraphy than by the same man's actions. Actions can be misleading. One can be trained to respond in a certain manner or to react with a certain emotion. Yet, one can not hide their heart when doing calligraphy. Here are the 8 ways of discerning a worthy hand:

1. An educated, refined hand is not forced. It must be free to move; without thought, only the emotion of the character should show through-- a balance between the purity of construction and effortless flow.

2. If you do not practice with an unclouded mind, the Truth that the ancients achieved will not be in your writings. It will only be smears of ink, scribbles with no feeling and no meaning. Such things will leave the

ardent lovers of calligraphy much saddened and disheartened.

3. No matter how fine the paper, if the hand is untrained and the mind clouded, all efforts are wasted.

4. Conversely, if one has practiced and truly understands the art of ink and brush, even a dull stone or scrap of wood can be made more beautiful than a finely made leaf of silk mounted on a brocade scroll or exotic stationary bound in an album with golden covers.

5. To copy Holy Scripture with a heart that begrudges the time spent before the venerable texts, is to pursue a ghost. Only when one's heart is centered upon the spirit of the texts does the Truth emerge from the pages.

6. If one can not write a character with at least five different emotions, then one is a poor calligrapher indeed. The character for dragon, for instance, can, with only minor nuances, be jubilant, proud, sorrowful, angry, or powerful.

7. If a student can not master all the ancient styles of calligraphy, then it is audacious of them to contemplate developing their own style. It is only through mastering the ancient styles that ones own hand grows capable enough to develop a style is both elegant and original.

8. The ultimate hallmark of a truly talented calligrapher is to be adept at seal carving. Each seal should be a masterwork which include all these traits;

impeccable form, shape of design, type of stone, an eye for choosing the right script, a knowledge of the archaic styles and all their variations, and a hand skillful at delicately carving the stone.

Poetry

My soul needs poetry the same way my lungs need air. Sadly, I am a fan of poetry, but not a composer there of. My poems are unoriginal and lack a vitality that is a must to be considered great. This is fine, for I am much contented to read the poems of the ancients.

My heart aches and my soul stirs as I read verses written a thousand years before I was born. Visions of misty valleys, endless mountains, unfathomed seas and clouds stretch out before me. Handsome scholars, drunken immortals, bawdy poets, and fine ladies appear one by one and guide me through a world that I surely knew in some past life. Otherwise, why should I feel so nostalgic for that bygone time?

When a person can not enjoy poetry, there is something gravely amiss in their life. A poem is a flower, with an enticing perfume, deeply colored petals, and hidden depths. It should be a world within a world-- a universe unto itself. What heart could be left cold by peering into that miniature world and finding itself there in some wild, lonesome landscape? Show me a man you who does not enjoy poetry and I will show you an uncouth dolt or a crass witling.

The Summerhouse of Infinite Joy

A poem written after reading Ben Wu's book the Summer House of Infinite Joy

>The tall pines sing,
>Two birds take wing,
>And the wind with blossoms toy.
>
>In sleep you'll dream,
>By the starry stream,
>That flows through the Garden of Infinite Joy.

An Inscription

Written as a forward for Ben Wu's book, Twenty Views of Living in Seclusion in late 2008

    The words and images herein touched my old heart in a very profound way. Mr. Ben Wu reveals the joys and loneliness of a life lived behind the Iron Threshold-- a life of books and daydreams; a life of strictness, yet freedom from society's constraints. Also, at the heart of this book is this revelation:

    To seek knowledge is not enough. Great truths must be pondered in contemplative silence. For, only in quietude can the flowers of thought bright forth the fruits of sagacity.

    Best wishes,
    Madame Li

Expounding the Classics

I was fortunate enough to be raised in a family that felt it was vital to educate the daughters as well as the sons. Of course my brother received more formal education than my sister and i, yet we were schooled thoroughly in the ancient classics. I was weaned on the Four Books for Women, Lao Tzu, Master Kong (Confucius), Meng Ko of Zou (Mencius), The Record of the Grand Historian, and all the other volumes that one must know to be considered learned. I read classic novels, hefty tomes on calligraphy, plays, songs, and volumes of poems, books on Buddhism, Taoism, manuals on herbs and medicine, and much more. Yet, I know I did not read enough to truly be called a scholar. I knew instinctively that my education was not balanced. I knew much of my people, our history and culture, but I knew nothing of the outside world. The land beyond the dragon's reach was a mystery to me. Great clouds of ignorance settled in the valleys of my mind...only distant misty peaks were visible. Immense cities of truth, paths of enlightenment, and sage immortals existed in the void that my thoughts could not penetrate.

Once older and in the leisure days of my life, I made a point to study all that the West considered classics. I asked some of my neighbors what I should read. The most often recommended book was the Bible. Others said Moby Dick, Pride and Prejudice, 2001: A Space Odyssey, Black Boy, To Kill a Mocking Bird, Atlas Shrugged, 1984, The Lord of the Rings, and a myriad of other books that made their way onto my list. I read them all.

Yet, I still consider myself but a simpleton when it comes to knowing man and his place in the world. I do not even fully understand myself and my place in the grand scheme of things. In fact after reading some 10,000 books in my life, I find that I have more questions than answers. This was the effect desired by the authors of the Classics. Those great thinkers of the ages want us to ponder truths and lies and ask ourselves the questions that we daren't ask. Some author's give us explanations for the mysteries that haunt the minds of men; they interject opinions and pose theories, but know in the end it is the reader that must decide.

We all would do well to read as much as possible of the ancients, but let us not forget the writers of our own time. We must listen to the wisdom of our peerage. They are not in some distant pavilion in some ancient time, but they sit in our midst, in an office cubical, in a college library, or in some coffee house. They ponder the questions of our times, offer theories and possibilities. They dream and sing and spout poetry and prose.

The classics of the ancient world are a foundation; the classics of our time are a temple in which we worship knowledge and the truths of our time. In time our novels and histories will be paved over and new temples will be erected and new truths will be enshrined. Other thinkers will read our words and the words of those that came before. Our words and our times will inspire new dreamers to dream of the far, distant future-- which will mirror an idyllic and imagined past that the classics evoke.

Final Thoughts from Madame Li

I did not intend to write so much and I hope you do not feel I have been heavy-handed. That was not the intention. I only wished to share with you the few morsels of knowledge that I have gathered in the last one hundred years

Until we meet again,

Acknowledgments

Madame Li would like to acknowledge the following:

My grand, grand nephew Yan: You have been my arms and legs since you were young. You have opened unto me a door to the whole world, via the internet. You have given so much of your time helping a silly old woman to pursue her folly and dreams; for that I thank you humbly.

To Ben Wu: I have long written journals and pondered all things great and small, yet , without your gentle urging and tireless assistance, this book would not have been made possible.

Chelsea Flattery: My gratefulness to this young lady is endless. Not only did she donate her immense talent as a writer, but she made a foolish old recluse sound like a sage advisor of men and keen observer of mankind. Thank you, my dear.

Sara Bean: You have been of a great help in editing and completing this writing project. I thank you humbly from the bottom of my heart.

Anya Kholodova: Your work on this book's cover left me in awe. Thank you so much for sharing your talents so generously.

Rebecca Ridout: I thank you for your kind assistance in my time of need.

A Note from Ben Wu

For the last few years, both artistically and personally, I have been encouraged and inspired by Madame Li. She has been both my mentor and my muse. In my mind she seemed to be a holy icon. Yet, she is not a distant saintly figure watching from some golden window, she is an old familiar friend. Someone to whom, I can turn for advice and for comfort when I am weary and worn. She both nurtures and reprimands with the gentle heart and compassion of a mother.

By compiling this book, I hope to share with the world and preserve for future generations the gentle voice and timeless wisdom of this grand, sage woman. I deserve no praise or lauding for this undertaking. Madame Li is the source and I am but a conduit. So, if you have any praise to give, heap it upon her worthy head. If you have any complaints, lay them at my door. Her words are flawless, but my skills as an editor are somewhat less than perfect.

Sincerely,
Ben Wu

www.ingramcontent.com/pod-product-compliance
Lightning Source LLC
Chambersburg PA
CBHW051708040426
42446CB00008B/784